ORNAMENTAL CARTOUCHES

BY
JOHANN ULRICH KRAUSS

Dover Publications, Inc., New York

PUBLISHER'S NOTE

Elegant and susceptible to great flights of imagination, the cartouche was given its most impressive interpretations in the seventeenth and eighteenth centuries. The 74 cartouches reproduced in this volume were created by Johann Ulrich Krauss (1655–1719) of Augsburg, Germany, as part of his *Historische Bilder-Bibel*. They reflect many influences of the period, especially those of French sources, and demonstrate the richness of late Baroque design. To facilitate their use by the modern artist and designer, the illustrations originally contained within the cartouches have been deleted.

Copyright © 1988 by Dover Publications, Inc.

All rights reserved under Pan American and International Copyright Conventions.

Published in Canada by General Publishing Company, Ltd., 30 Lesmill Road, Don Mills, Toronto, Ontario.

Published in the United Kingdom by Constable and Company, Ltd.

This Dover edition, first published in 1988, is a selection of cartouches from Johann Ulrich Krauss's *Historische Bilder-Bibel*, originally published by the artist in Augsburg in five parts between 1698 and 1700. For the present edition, pictorial material originally contained within the cartouches has been deleted.

DOVER *Pictorial Archive* SERIES

Manufactured in the United States of America
Dover Publications, Inc., 31 East 2nd Street, Mineola, N.Y. 11501

Library of Congress Cataloging-in-Publication Data

Krauss, Johann Ulrich, 1645–1719.
 Ornamental cartouches.

 (Dover pictorial archive series)
 A selection of cartouches from artist's Historische Bilder-Bibel.
 1. Cartouches, Ornamental (Decorative arts) 2. Decoration and ornament, Baroque. I. Krauss, Johann Ulrich, 1645–1719. Historische Bilder-Bibel. II. Title. III. Series.
 NK1585.K7 1988   745.4'43   88-3629
 ISBN 0-486-25665-0 (pbk.)

3

9

14

22

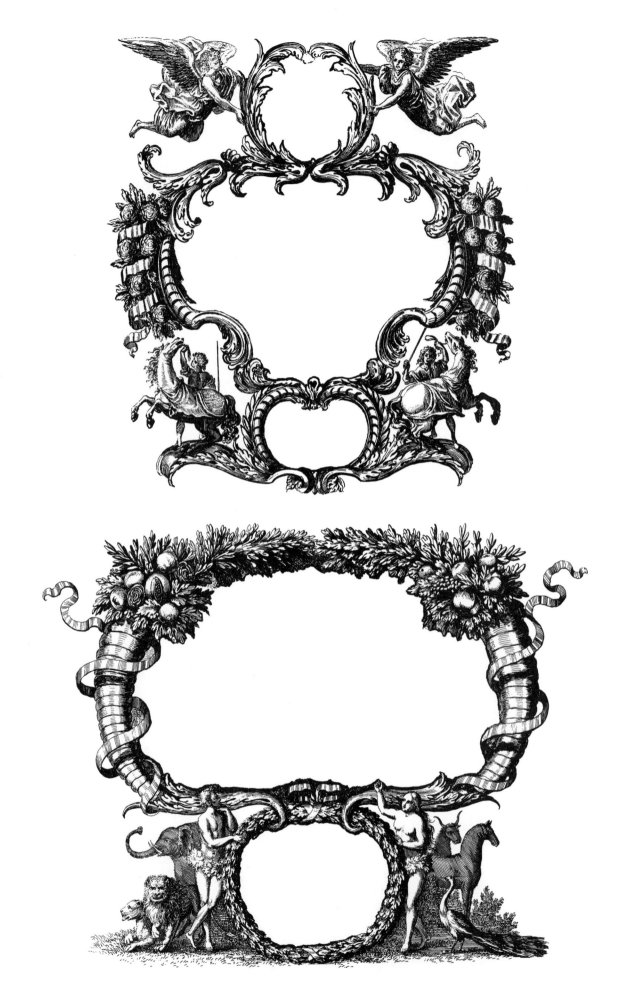

34

41